Rust Programming in Examples
(Beginners Guide)

Table of Contents

Introduction

Systems programming has always been viewed as a tough area in Computer Science. It involves the development of applications capable of operating closely to the computer hardware compared to application-level applications which users directly interact with. The development of systems program requires a programming language capable of supporting concurrency. The Rust programming language is a language that was developed to be used in systems programming. The language has a strong support for concurrency which makes it suitable for use in systems programming. The language has a simple syntax, similar to that of C++ but with only few differences. If you are familiar5 with C++, then it is easy for you to learn Rust. This book is an excellent guide for you on how to program in Rust. The author takes you through a step-by-step process in order to learn Rust. Enjoy reading!

Chapter 1- Getting Started with Rust

Rust is a modern programming language that focuses on speed, safety and concurrency. These goals are achieved by not using garbage collection, which in turn makes it memory safe.

Installing Rust

The installation and management of rust is done using the rustup tool. It runs on various platforms, so there are various builds of rust at any time. The rustup tool manages the builds in a very consistent manner on each platform that is supported by Rust. This facilitates the installation of Rust from beta and nightly release channels and the support for the additional cross-compilation targets.

The rustup tool normally installs rustc, cargo, rustup as well as other standard tools to the Cargo's bin directory. On Windows, this can be found at "%USERPROFILE%\.cargo\bin" while on UNIX, it can be found at "$HOME/.cargo/bin". Rust programs and Cargo plugins will also be installed in the same directory.

The directory should be in your $PATH environment variable, which will make it possible for you to run them from the shell with no need for a further configuration.

On Windows, you just have to download the rustup-init.exe file then launch it by double clicking it. The installation will begin and you should follow the instructions as shown on the command prompt of your Windows operating system. Once the installation is done, run the following command on the command prompt to check the version that is running on your system:

rustc –version

This should print the version of Rust running on your system. If the command fails to run, then you must re-install the tool.

```
C:\Users\admin>rustc --version
rustc 1.21.0 (3b72af97e 2017-10-09)

C:\Users\admin>
```

Anytime that you need to uninstall the tool from your system, just run the following command:

rustup self uninstall

Hello World Program

Here is the "Hello World" example in Rust:

fn main() {

    // Print text the console
    println!("Hello World!");
}

The first line of the code denotes the main function. To print text to the console, we have used the "println!()" function. Note that the line ends with a semicolon (;). The file with the code should be saved with a ".rs" extension to mark it as a rust file.

We can use the Rust compiler (rustc) in order to generate a binary from the above code. We just have to call the compiler plus the name of the file as shown below:

rustc hello.rs

The command will create a binary code from the "hello.rs" file, and the binary will be named "hello". To execute it, we can run the following command:

./hello

7

Note that the command begins with a "./", that is, a dot and a forward slash. The code should print "Hello World!" on the console.

Comments

Comments are essential in any programming language including Rust. Let us discuss the various types of comments supported in Rust:

1. Regular Comments
   These are ignored by the compiler. To mark a line as a comment, we preceed it with two forward slashes, that is, //. Example:
   // Line comment
   Block comments normally exceed a line. They are marked as follows:
   /*Block comments */

2. Doc Comments
   These are parsed into HTML library. Example:

   /// Generate library docs for the following item.

   //! Generate library docs for enclosing item.

Chapter 2- Primitives

Rust provides various types of primitives. Let us discuss them.

Literals and Operators

Integers, floats, characters, Booleans, strings and unit type can be expressed by use of literals. Alternatively, integers can be expressed by use of hexadecimals binary or octal notation using any of 0x, 0o or 0b prefixes.
We can add underscores to numerical literals for the purpose of improving readability. Example, 2_000 is similar to 2000, and 0.000_001 is similar to 0.000001.

The compiler should be told of the type of literal that we have used. We can use the u32 suffix as an indication that we have an unsigned 32-bit integer and i32 to indicate that we have a signed 32 bit integer. Rust has the same operators as those used in c-like languages and their order of precedence remains to be the same. Consider the example given below:

```
fn main() {
    // Adding Integers
    println!("2 + 3 = {}", 2u32 + 3);

    // Subtracting Integers
    println!("2 - 3 = {}", 2i32 - 3);

    // Try to change `1i32` to `1u32` and see the
importance of type

    // Short-circuiting boolean logic
    println!("false AND true is {}", false && true);
    println!("true OR false is {}", true || false);
    println!("NOT true is {}", !true);
    // Bitwise operations

    println!("0011 AND 0101 is {:04b}", 0b0011u32 &
0b0101);
```

```
    println!("0011 OR 0101 is {:04b}", 0b0011u32 |
0b0101);

    println!("0011 XOR 0101 is {:04b}", 0b0011u32 ^
0b0101);

    println!("1 << 5 is {}", 1u32 << 5);
    println!("0x80 >> 2 is 0x{:x}", 0x80u32 >> 2);

    // Underscores for improving readability

    println!("Two hundred thousand can be written as
{}", 200_000u32);
}
```

The above code should give the following output:

```
2 + 3 = 5
2 - 3 = -1
false AND true is false
true OR false is true
NOT true is false
0011 AND 0101 is 0001
0011 OR 0101 is 0111
0011 XOR 0101 is 0110
1 << 5 is 32
0x80 >> 2 is 0x20
Two hundred thousands can be written as 200000
```

Consider the following line extracted from the program:
println!("2 + 3 = {}", 2u32 + 3);

We have the "println!()" function. The first part of the function contents, that is, "2 + 3 = {}", has been enclosed within quotes. The part will be printed as it is. The second part, that is, 2u32 + 3, has not been enclosed, and it will give the sum of 2 and 3, which is 5. The u32 denotes that we have an unsigned 32 bit integer.

In the next part, we have Boolean operations, false AND true gives a false, while true OR false gives a true. That is how we can work with literals and apply operators on them.

Tuples

A tuple store values of different types. They are created using parenthesis (), and every tuple itself is a value with type signature (T1, T2, ...), in which the T1, T2... are types of its members. Tuples are useful to functions when they need to return multiple values since the tuples are able to hold any number of values. Example:

// Tuples may be used as function arguments as well as return values

```
fn reverse(pair: (i32, bool)) -> (bool, i32) {
// `let` can be used for binding members of a tuple to the variables

    let (integer, boolean) = pair;

    (boolean, integer)
}

// The struct for the activity.
#[derive(Debug)]
struct Matrix(f32, f32, f32, f32);

fn main() {
    // A tuple holding different types
    let tuple1 = (1u8, 2u16, 3u32, 4u64,
            -1i8, -2i16, -3i32, -4i64,
            0.1f32, 0.2f64,
            'a', true);

    // We can use tuple indexing to extract values from the tuple
```

```rust
    println!("First value for tuple1: {}", tuple1.0);
    println!("Second value for tuple1: {}", tuple1.1);

    // Tuples may be tuple members
    let tuple2 = ((1u8, 2u16, 2u32), (4u64, -1i8), -2i16);

    // Tuples can be printed
    println!("Tuple of tuples: {:?}", tuple2);

    // However, long Tuples cannot be printed
    // let too_long_tuple = (1, 2, 3, 4, 5, 6, 7, 8, 9, 10, 11,
12, 13);
    // println!("too long tuple: {:?}", too_long_tuple);

    // Uncomment the above 2 lines and see compiler
error

    let pair = (1, true);
    println!("Pair is {:?}", pair);

    println!("Reversed pair gives {:?}", reverse(pair));

    // When creating one element tuples, we use a
comma to tell them apart

    // from literal surrounded by parentheses
    println!("A tuple with one element: {:?}", (10u32,));
    println!("Simply an integer: {:?}", (10u32));

    //We can deconstruct tuples to create bindings
    let tuple = (1, "hello", 4.5, true);

    let (a, b, c, d) = tuple;
    println!("{:?}, {:?}, {:?}, {:?}", a, b, c, d);

    let matrix = Matrix(1.1, 1.2, 2.1, 2.2);
    println!("{:?}", matrix);
```

}

When executed, the program should give the following result:

```
First value for tuple1: 1
Second value for tuple1: 2
Tuple of tuples: ((1, 2, 2), (4, -1), -2)
Pair is (1, true)
Reversed pair gives (true, 1)
A tuple with one element: (10,)
Simply an integer: 10
1, "hello", 4.5, true
Matrix(1.1, 1.2, 2.1, 2.2)
```

We have used the "let" keyword to create a tuple named "tuple1" in the following line:

let tuple1 = (1u8, 2u16, 3u32, 4u64, -1i8, -2i16, -3i32, -4i64, 0.1f32, 0.2f64, 'a', true);

We have then used the dot (.) operator to access the values contained in the tuple. We have accessed the element, which is at index 0 and the second element which is at index 1. This means that the elements of an array begin at index 0.

We have then created the tuple named "tuple2", and this is a tuple of tuples. The call to the "reverse ()" function prints the elements of "pair" in a reversed format, meaning that the printing will begin from the last to the first element. Note that a comma (,) has been used when defining a tuple with one element.

Arrays and Slices

Unlike a tuple, an array is used to store elements of the same type in a contiguous memory. The declaration of arrays is done using square brackets and their size must be stated. However, the size of the array is known during compile time. Array is declared by following the type signature given below:

[T; size]

Where T represents the types of the array elements followed by the array size. Slices are just like arrays, but their size is not known during the compile time.
A slice is just a two-word object, with the first word acting as the pointer to the data, while the second word points to the length of the slice. The word size is similar to the usize and it is determined by the architecture of the processor. They can be used when we need to borrow only a section of an array. Slices take the following type signature:

&[T]

Consider the following example:

```
use std::mem;

// This function borrows a slice
fn analyze_slice(slice: &[i32]) {
    println!("first element of the slice: {}", slice[0]);
    println!("The slice has {} elements", slice.len());
}

fn main() {
    // Array witha  fixed size
    let array1: [i32; 5] = [1, 2, 3, 4, 5];

    // We can initialize all the elements to the same value

    let array2: [i32; 500] = [0; 500];
```

```rust
    // Indexing begins at 0
    println!("First element of array1: {}", array1[0]);
    println!("Second element of array1: {}", array1[1]);

    // `len` givess the size of array
    println!("Array size: {}", array1.len());
    // Arrays are stack allocated
    println!("Array occupies {} bytes",
mem::size_of_val(&array1));

    // Arrays can be borrowed automatically as slices
    println!("Borrow the whole of the array as a slice");
    analyze_slice(&array2);

    // Slices can point to part of an array
    println!("Borrow part of the array as slice");
    analyze_slice(&array2[1 .. 4]);

    // Out of bound indexing gives panic
    println!("{}", array1[5]);
}
```

The program should give the following result when executed:

```
First element of array1: 1
Second element of array1: 2
Array size: 5
Array occupies 20 bytes
Borrow the whole of the array as a slice
first element of the slice: 0
The slice has 500 elements
Borrow part of the array as slice
first element of the slice: 0
The slice has 3 elements
```

We have used the "let" keyword to define our first array named "array1". To Access the elements of the array, we must place the index of the element within the square brackets.

The array named "array2" will have a total of 500 elements and all the elements will be of the same value. The "len()" function returns the length of the array. The "[1 .. 4]" helps us to borrow the elements of the array of the array whose indices lie within the specified indices.

Chapter 3- Variables

Variables point to a memory location in which a particular value is stored. To declare variables in Rust, we use the "let" keyword as shown below:

let x = 10;

The "let" keyword is used for declaration of local variables in Rust. You also notice that there is no explicit declaration of the type of variable in the above declaration. However, we have assigned an integer value to the variable, that is, 10. The compiler will automatically infer that the variable is an int. However, sometimes, the compiler can conclude wrongly. This is why it is good for you to state the type of the variable you are declaring. This can be done as demonstrated below:

let x: int = 10;

Note that when declaring a variable, the = sign is used for assignment purposes. The statement has also been terminated using a semicolon (;). To finalize this, the declaration of variables in Rust is done using the following syntax:

let name[: type] [= value];

The items placed in the brackets are optional.

Variable Bindings

Rust employs the mechanism of static typing in order to provide type safety. The variable bindings may be type annotated during the declaration. Example:

```
fn main() {
    let num = 1u32;
    let bool = true;
    let unit = ();
```

```
// copy `num` into `num2`
let num2 = num;

println!("An integer: {:?}", num2);
println!("A boolean: {:?}", bool);
println!("The unit value: {:?}", unit);

// The compiler will warn about unused variable
bindings. We can silence the warnings

//by prefixing the variable name with underscore
let _unused_var = 5u32;

let noisy_unused_var = 1u32;

// Prefix it with an underscore to suppress the
warning
}
```

The program should give the following result when executed:

```
An integer: 1
A boolean: true
The unit value: ()
```

That is how variables can be declared in Rust. After executing the program, you will get a warning about the last variable. This is because it is noisy. You will also be asked to prefix it with an underscore in order to suppress the warning.

Mutability

In Rust, the variable bindings are immutable by default. However, we can use the "mut" identifier in order to override this. Example:

```rust
fn main() {
    let _immutable = 2;
    let mut mutable = 2;

    println!("Before mutation: {}", mutable);

    // Ok
    mutable += 1;

    println!("After mutation: {}", mutable);

    // This will give an error
    _immutable += 1;
    // Comment out the above line to solve the error
}
```

Once executed, the above program will give an error. To remove the error, you just have to comment out the following line:

_immutable += 1;

The program will then give the following result once executed:

```
Before mutation: 2
After mutation: 3
```

Note that we have used the "mut" keyword to make the variable mutable. We have changed the value of the variable by adding 1 to its initial value of 2, which gives us three.

Scope and Shadowing

In Rust, variable bindings have a scope, and they are constrained to live within a block. A block refers to a collection of statements that are enclosed within braces {}. Variable shadowing is also allowed, which is a property in which the same name is used to declare variables located in different scopes. Consider the example given below:

```
fn main() {
    // This binding will live in main function
    let bigger_scope = 1;

    // This is a block with a smaller scope than our main function
    {
        // This binding will only be acessible from within this block

        let short_scope = 2;

        println!("Inner short: {}", short_scope);

        // This binding will shadow the outer one
        let bigger_scope = 5_f32;

        println!("Inner long: {}", bigger_scope);
    }
    // Block end.

    // Error! `short_scope` doesn't exist in this scope
    println!("Outer short: {}", short_scope);
    // Comment out the above line to solve the error

    println!("Outer long: {}", bigger_scope);

    // This binding will also shadow the previous binding

    let bigger_scope = 'a';
```

println!("Outer long: {}", bigger_scope);
}

Run the code and you will get an error about the following line:

println!("Outer short: {}", short_scope);

This is because the variable is not within that scope. The variable "short_scope" has been defined within the block enclosed within braces {}, hence it is only accessible from within that block. Trying to access it from outside that block will give an error. To remove the error, you can comment out the line. The program will then give the following result once executed:

```
Inner short: 2
Inner long: 5
Outer long: 1
Outer long: a
```

Chapter 4- Type Casting

In Rust, there are several ways of changing the type and defining the primitives and the user defined types.

In Rust, coercion or implicit type conversion is not supported between primitive types. However, we can perform type casting/ explicit type conversion by use of the "as" keyword. Example:

```
// Suppress all the warnings from overflowing casts
#![allow(overflowing_literals)]

fn main() {
    let decimalNum = 34.4147_f32;

    // Error! No implicit conversion
    let integerNum: u8 = decimalNum;
    // Comment out the above line to solve the error

    // Explicit conversion
    let integerNum = decimalNum as u8;
    let character = integerNum as char;

    println!("Type Casting: {} -> {} -> {}", decimalNum,
integerNum, character);

    // when casting a value to unsigned type, T,
    // std::T::MAX + 1 should be added or subtracted
until the value

    // fits into new type

    // 1000 fits in a u16
    println!("1000 in the form of u16 is: {}", 1000 as
u16);

    // 1000 - 256 - 256 - 256 = 232
    // The first 8 least significant bits will be kept,
```

// while the rest towards the most significant bit will be truncated.

```
    println!("1000 in the form of u8 is : {}", 1000 as u8);
    // -1 + 256 = 255
    println!(" -1 as a u8 is : {}", (-1i8) as u8);

    // For positive numbers, it is similar to the modulus
    println!("1000 mod 256 is : {}", 1000 % 256);

    println!(" 128 in the form of i16 is: {}", 128 as i16);
    // 128 as u8 -> 128, with a two's complement in eight bits of:
    println!(" 128 as a i8 is : {}", 128 as i8);

    // repeating the above example
    // 1000 as u8 -> 232
    println!("1000 in the form of  u8 is : {}", 1000 as u8);
    // The two's complement for 232 is -24
    println!(" 232 in the form of i8 is : {}", 232 as i8);
}
```

Run the program and you will get an error. To solve out this, you should comment out the following line of code:

let integerNum: u8 = decimalNum;
The program should then execute successfully to give out the following error:

```
Type Casting: 34.4147 -> 34 -> "
1000 in the form of u16 is: 1000
1000 in the form of u8 is : 232
  -1 as a u8 is : 255
1000 mod 256 is : 232
 128 in the form of i16 is: 128
 128 as a i8 is : -128
1000 in the form of  u8 is : 232
 232 in the form of i8 is : -24
```

It is very clear that implicit type conversion is not supported in Rust. Explicit type conversion has been done in the following lines:

let integerNum = decimalNum as u8;
let character = integerNum as char;

Chapter 5- Flow Control

Every programming language should have mechanisms of controlling how the execution of statements is done. Rust ha statements have statements that can be used for the control of flow of execution.

If

The "if" statement is used to evaluate a particular condition, after which various decisions may be made. In this case, we have a single choice leading to two paths as demonstrated below:

```
fn main() {
  let p = 10;

if p == 10 {
    println!("P is Ten!");
}
}
```

The program would print the statement. This is because the condition under evaluation has been met. If the value of the variable is changed, the statement will not be printed. This is because the condition has not been met, and we have not defined what to do in case this case. The logic behind the "if" statement is simple, if the expression under "if" is true; the block is executed, if false, the block is not executed.

if/else

In our previous example, there was nothing to be done in case the "if" expression is false.

This can be used by using "else" statement. Example:

```
fn main() {
  let p = 17;
```

```
if p == 10 {
  println!("p is 10");
} else {
  println!("p is not ten");

  };
}
```

The block under the else part will be executed; hence, you will see the print statement below it printed.

Sometimes, we may be in need of evaluating several decisions. This calls for us to use "else if" statement. The following example demonstrates this:

```
fn main() {
  let p = 10;

  if p < 0 {
    print!("{} is negative", p);
  } else if p > 0 {
    print!("{} is positive", p);
  } else {
    print!("{} is zero", p);
  }

  let big_p =
    if p < 10 && p > -10 {
      println!(", and is a small number, multiply by ten");
      // The expression will return an `i32`.
      10 * p
    } else {
      println!(", and is a big number, divide by two");

      // The expression must return an `i32`
      p / 2
      // Try to suppress the expression with a
semicolon.
```

```
};
    println!("{} -> {}", p, big_p);
}
```

The program gives the following output:

```
10 is positive, and is a big number, divide by two
10 -> 5
```

Consider the following statement extracted from the program:

if p < 10 && p > -10 {

We have used the && (AND) operator to evaluate the value of p. The statement simply checks whether "the value of p is between -10 and 10". If met, its block will be executed.

Chapter 6- Loops

Rust provides us with three ways of performing iterative tasks. These include the "loop", the "while" and the "for". Let us discuss them.

Loop

This infinite loop is the simplest form of loop in Rust. When using the "loop" keyword, Rust allows us to loop iteratively until a particular terminating condition is met. It can be used as shown below:

```
loop {
    println!("Loop without stopping");
}
```

The program will run without stopping. You just have to add the statements to be executed within the block of the loop.

While

With the "while" loop, the statements will be executed as long as the condition specified in the "while" condition is true. The following example demonstrates this:

```
fn main() {
    let mut p = 10;
let mut done = false;

while !done {
    p += p - 3;

    println!("{}", p);
    if p % 5 == 0 {
        done = true;
    }
}
}
```

The program gives the following result when executed:

```
17
31
59
115
```

The condition:

while !done

Will be evaluated and as long as it is true, the statements below it will be executed. In the statement:

if p % 5 == 0

We have used the modulus (%) operator to determine the remainder after dividing the value of p by 5. If the remainder is zero (0), then the value of "done" will be true.

This type of loop is the best for you to use whenever you are not sure of the number of times that you should loop. If you are in need of an infinite loop, then you can write the following:

while true {

However, this can be easily be handled using the "loop" statement discussed above.

For

This type of loop is used when we need to loop for a number of times. However, the "for" loop in Rust works a bit differently compared to other programming languages. It takes the following syntax:

```
for var in expression {
    code
}
```

The following example demonstrates this:

```
for p in 0..10 {
    println!("{}", p); // p: i32
}
```

The iteration in the syntax given above is simply an item that can be converted into an integer by use of the IntoIterator. The iterator in turn gives back a series of items, one item for every iteration of the loop. The value will then be bound to the variable "var", and this is valid for loop body. After the body is over, the next value will be fetched from the iterator, and then we will loop again. However, the upper bound is not included, so our above code will print values from 0 to 9. When the loop does not have any more values, it will terminate.

Consider the final example given below:

```
fn main() {
    let mut count = 0u32;
    println!("Count to infinity!");

    // An infinite loop
    loop {
        count += 1;

        if count == 4 {
            println!("Count at four");

            // Skip the rest of the iteration
            continue;
        }

        println!("{}", count);
```

```
    if count == 7 {
        println!("OK, we have counted enough");

        // Exit the loop
        break;
    }
  }
}
```

The program should give the result shown below once executed:

```
Count to infinity!
1
2
3
Count at four
5
6
7
OK, we have counted enough
```

Note that we have skipped the count when 4 is reached. The "break" statement has then been used to terminate the loop once the value of the count is 7.

Enumerate

When you are in need of knowing the number of times that you have iterated, you can use the ".enumerate ()" function. Consider the following example:

```
fn main() {
  for (index, value) in (5..10).enumerate() {
    println!("index = {} with value = {}", index, value);
  }
}
```

This will give the following result:

```
index = 0 with value = 5
index = 1 with value = 6
index = 2 with value = 7
index = 3 with value = 8
index = 4 with value = 9
```

We have used the "index" variable in order to track the number of times we have iterated.

Nesting Loops

Rust supports the use of nested loops. These can be used together with the "break" or "continue". In such cases, the loops should have a 'label and the label should be passed to the break/continue statement. Example:

#![allow(unreachable_code)]

```
fn main() {
  'outer: loop {
    println!("This is the outer loop");

    'inner: loop {
      println!("This is the inner loop");

      // This wwill break only inner loop
      //break;

      // This will break the outer loop
      break 'outer;
    }

    println!("The loops will not reach this point");
  }

  println!("Outer loop Exited!");
}
```

The program will give the following result when executed:

```
This is the outer loop
This is the inner loop
Outer loop Exited!
```

That is how loops can be nested.

Chapter 7- Functions

To declare functions in Rust, we use the "fn" keyword. The arguments to the function are type annotated in the same way as variables, and in case the function returns a value, the return type should be specified after the arrow ->.

Every program in Rust has at least one function, that is, the "main" function:

```
fn main() {
}
```

The "fn" function states that we are creating a function. This is followed by the name of the function "main" and the parenthesis since the function takes no arguments. The curly braces {} declare the body of the function. Here is an example of another function:

```
fn foo() {
}
```

The function takes no arguments. However, it is possible for us to define a Rust function that takes arguments. This is demonstrated below:

```
fn print_integer(p: i32) {
    println!("p is: {}", p);
}
```

The above function will look for the value of the variable p from within the program and print it on the terminal. The complete program for the function can be written as follows:

```
fn main() {
    print_integer(20);
}

fn print_integer(p: i32) {
```

```
    println!("p is: {}", p);
}
```

When executed, the program will print the following output:

```
p is: 20
```

As show in the above example, the function arguments work in the same way as the "let" declarations. A type must be added to the argument name after the colon. Consider the example given below:

```
fn main() {
    print_sum(10, 20);
}

fn print_sum(p: i32, q: i32) {
    println!("The sum is: {}", p + q);
}
```

When executed, the program will give the result shown below:

```
The sum is: 30
```

We have declared the function named "print_sum". Two integer arguments, 10 and 20, have been passed to the function.
We are then getting the sum of these two arguments and then print their sum on the terminal.

Note that arguments should be separated using a semicolon both during the declaration and when calling them.

However, unlike what we have in *let*, the type of the arguments must be specified. Consider the example given below:

```
fn print_sum(p, q) {
    println!("The sum is: {}", p + q);
```

```
}
```

The above example will give an error. For the case of declaring variables with *let,* the type could be inferred automatically after the assignment. This is not the case like when declaring functions. Consider the example given below:

```
fn main() {
    fizzbuzz_to(100);
}

// returns a boolean value
fn is_divisible_by(lhs: u32, rhs: u32) -> bool {
    // Corner case, an early return
    if rhs == 0 {
        return false;
    }

    // An expression, the `return` keyword isn't necessary

    lhs % rhs == 0
}
// Functions not returning a value, actually it returns
the unit type `()`

fn fizzbuzz(n: u32) -> () {
    if is_divisible_by(n, 15) {
        println!("fizzbuzz");
    } else if is_divisible_by(n, 3) {
        println!("fizz");
    } else if is_divisible_by(n, 5) {
        println!("buzz");
    } else {
        println!("{}", n);
    }
}
```

```
// The return type may be omitted from the signature
since the function returns `()'

fn fizzbuzz_to(n: u32) {
    for n in 1..n + 1 {
        fizzbuzz(n);
    }
}
```

Run the program then observe the output that you get.

Methods

Functions are good, but it can be awkward when you need to call many of them on a particular data. Consider the code given below:

baz(bar(foo));

You will probably read the above from left to the right, that is, "baz bar foo". However, this is not the order by which functions are called. Functions are called using the inside-out approach, that is, "foo bar baz". It will be nice if we do it as follows:

baz(bar(foo));

Rust supports the use of the above method syntax by use of the "impl" syntax.

Method Calls

In Rust, method calls can be implemented as follows:

```
struct Circle {
    radius: f64,
    x: f64,
    y: f64,
```

```
}

impl Circle {
  fn getArea(&self) -> f64 {
    std::f64::consts::PI * (self.radius * self.radius)
  }
}

fn main() {
  let circ = Circle { x: 0.0, y: 0.0, radius: 2.0 };

  println!("{}", circ.getArea());
}
```

This will print the value of area. We began by creating a struct to represent a circle. We have then created an "impl" block and the method "getArea" has been defined inside it. The first method in a method is special, and there are three variants of this. They include "self", "&self", and "&mut self". In the foo.bar (), this parameter can be thought as the foo. The three variants of the first parameter correspond to what foo could be. For "self" when it is a value on the stack, "&self" when it is a reference and "&mut self" when it is a mutable reference. Since we took the "&self" parameter to the area, it can be used as any other parameter. Since we are aware that it is a circle, the radius can be accessed in the same way any other struct can be accessed.

It is recommended we default into using &self since it is good to prefer borrowing that taking ownership and taking immutable references over the mutable ones. The three variants can be used as follows:

```
#![allow(unused_variables)]
fn main() {
struct Circle {
  radius: f64,
  x: f64,
  y: f64,
```

```
}

impl Circle {
  fn byReference(&self) {
    println!("Self by reference");
  }

  fn byMutableReference(&mut self) {
    println!("Self by mutable reference");
  }

  fn byTakingOwnership(self) {
    println!("Taking ownership of self");
  }
}
}
```

You can use as many "impl" blocks as you need. With this, we can write our previous example as follows:

```
#![allow(unused_variables)]
fn main() {
struct Circle {
  radius: f64,
  x: f64,
  y: f64,

}

impl Circle {
  fn reference(&self) {
    println!("Self by reference");
  }
}

impl Circle {
  fn mutable_reference(&mut self) {
    println!("Self by mutable reference");
```

```rust
    }
}

impl Circle {
    fn takes_ownership(self) {
        println!("Taking ownership of self");
    }
}
}
```

Chapter 8- Traits

A trait is simply a language feature telling the Rust compiler about functionality that a type must provide. Remember how we used the "impl" keyword to call a function.

Traits are similar with the difference being that we have to define a trait with method signature, and then implement a trait for a type. In the example given below, we are implementing a trait named "HasArea" for "Circle":

struct Circle {

    radius: f64,
    x: f64,
    y: f64,

}

trait HasArea {
   fn area(&self) -> f64;
}

impl HasArea for Circle {
   fn area(&self) -> f64 {
     std::f64::consts::PI * (self.radius * self.radius)
   }
}

When observed keenly, you find that the "trait" block looks similar to the "impl" block, but a body is not defined. We only define a type signature. When implementing a trait, we normally use the "impl Trait for Item" instead of "impl Item".

We can use "self" in a type annotation in order to refer to an instance of type that is implementing this trait passed in the form of a parameter. The three variants of the first parameter may be used based on the level of ownership that is required:

```rust
struct Circle {
    radius: f64,
    x: f64,
    y: f64,

}

trait HasArea {
    fn area(&self) -> f64;

    fn is_larger(&self, &Self) -> bool;
}

impl HasArea for Circle {
    fn area(&self) -> f64 {
        std::f64::consts::PI * (self.radius * self.radius)
    }

    fn is_larger(&self, other: &Self) -> bool {
        self.area() > other.area()
    }
}
```

Chapter 9- Pattern Matching

The if/else" statement may not be applicable in all circumstances. The Rust programming language provides us with the "match" keyword that can help us to replace the complex if/else statements as well as in pattern matching. The "match" takes an expression and it then branches based on its values. Consider the example given below:

```
fn main() {
let p = 2;
match p {
   1 => println!("P is one"),
   2 => println!("P is two"),
   3 => println!("P is three"),
   4 => println!("P is four"),
   5 => println!("P is five"),
   _ => println!("P is something else"),
}
}
```

In the above example, the value of p will be matched against the various options. The second print statement will be printed on the terminal since a correct matching will occur there. Since its value matches, its corresponding expression is evaluated.

Since "match" is an expression, it can be used on the right-hand side of a "let" binding or directly where we are using an expression. Here is an example:

```
let p = 2;

let _number = match p {
   1 => println!("P is one"),
   2 => println!("P is two"),
   3 => println!("P is three"),
   4 => println!("P is four"),
   5 => println!("P is five"),
```

```
    _ => "P is something else",
};
```

It is a good way of converting something to something else. In our case, we have converted an integer into a string.

Consider the final example given below:

```
fn main() {
let position = 13;
// Try different values for `position`

println!("Tell me about {}", position);
match position {
// Matching a single value
1 => println!("Position is One!"),
// Match several values
2 | 3 | 5 | 7 | 11 => println!("Position is a prime
number"),
// Matching an inclusive range
13...19 => println!("Position represents a teen age"),
// The remaining cases
_ => println!("Position is something special"),
}

let boolean = true;
// Match is an expression
let binary = match boolean {
false => 0,
true => 1,
// Comment out one of the arms
};

println!("{} -> {}", boolean, binary);
}
```

This gives the following result when executed:

```
Tell me about 13
Position represents a teen age
true -> 1
```

As shown in the example, match can be used for the purpose of matching against several values. In such a case, the values should be separated using a | symbol.

Destructuring

In case of a compound data type such as a struct, it is possible for us to destruct it inside a pattern. Example:

fn main() {
  struct Coordinate {
  x: i32,
  y: i32,
}

let point = Coordinate { x: 10, y: 10 };

match point {
  Coordinate { x, y } => println!("({},{})", x, y),
}
}

In case we need to match a different name, we can use a colon (:) as follows:

struct Coordinate {
  x: i32,
  y: i32,
}

let point = Coordinate { x: 0, y: 0 };

match point {

```
    Coordinate { x: x1, y: y1 } => println!("({},{})", x1,
y1),
}
```

In case we are only concerned about some values, then there is no need for us to give all of them names. Example:

```
struct Coordinate {
    x: i32,
    y: i32,
}
```

```
let point = Coordinate { x: 2, y: 3 };
```

```
match point {
    Coordinate { x, .. } => println!("x is {}", x),
}
```
You will get the value of x as 2.

Chapter 10- Vectors

A vector refers to a "growable" and dynamic array that is implemented in the form of standard library type Vec<T>. The "T" is an indication that it is possible for us to have vectors of any type, In Vectors, data allocation is done on the heap. They can be created by use of the "vec!" macro as shown below:

let vector1 = vec![1, 2, 3, 4, 5];

We also have an alternative for vec! If we need to repeat the initial value:

let vector1 = vec![0; 10];

In vectors, the contents are stored in a contiguous array of T on heap. This is an indication they should be in a position to know the size of the T at compile time, that is, the number of bytes needed to store a T. We are unable to know the size of some things during the compile time. In such a case, a pointer to that thing should be stored.

Accessing Vector Elements

For us to access an element of a vector at a particular index, we use square brackets []. Example:

```
#![allow(unused_variables)]
fn main() {
let vector1 = vec![1, 2, 3, 4, 5];

println!("The second element in vector1 is {}",
vector1[1]);

}
```

In the above example, we have created a vector named "vector1" and we have stored numbers in it. We have then accessed the element stored at the index 1 of the array, and this will give us the second element in the array. Note that the first element in vector is at index 0.

Also, when indexing, remember to use the usize type as shown below:

let vector1 = vec![1, 2, 3, 4, 5];

let x: usize = 0;
let y: i32 = 0;

// This will work fine:
vector1[x];

// This will not work:
vector1[y];

Note that we used the i32 type for y, and that is why it won't work. When we index using a non-usize type, we normally get an error.

Consider the following example in which we are trying to access an element that doesn't exist:

let vector1 = vec![1, 2, 3];
println!("The content of index 6 is {}", vector1[6]);

In the above example, we are accessing the element stored at index 6, but this doesn't exist. The thread will panic with a message and it will be printed on the terminal.

If you are in need of handling out-of-bounds errors with no panicking, use methods such as "get" or "get_mut" that return "None" whenever given an invalid index. This is demonstrated below:

```rust
#![allow(unused_variables)]
fn main() {
let vector1 = vec![1, 2, 3];
match vector1.get(6) {
    Some(p) => println!("The item at index 6 is {}", p),
    None => println!("Sorry, not found. The vector is
too short.")
}

}
```

Since we are accessing an index that is not available, the last print statement will be printed on the terminal. That is how you can handle such errors.

Iteration

After creating your, you can use the "for" loop in order to iterate through its elements. There are three ways by which this can be done. These are demonstrated below:

```rust
#![allow(unused_variables)]
fn main() {
let mut vector1 = vec![1, 2, 3, 4, 5];

for x in &vector1 {
    println!("Referencing {}", x);
}

for x in &mut vector1 {
    println!("Mutable reference to {}", x);
}

for x in vector1 {
    println!("Taking ownership of vector and its
element {}", x);
}
}
```

Note that once you iterate a vector by taking ownership of the vector, it cannot be used again. If you need to iterate a vector multiple times, you just have to take a reference to the vector while iterating. Consider the code given below that will not compile:

```
let vector1 = vec![1, 2, 3, 4, 5];

for x in vector1 {
    println!(" Taking ownership of vector and its element  {}", x);
}

for x in vector1 {
    println!(" Taking ownership of vector and its element {}", x);
}
```

The following code will work perfectly:

```
#![allow(unused_variables)]
fn main() {
let vector1 = vec![1, 2, 3, 4, 5];

for x in &vector1 {
    println!("A reference to {}", x);
}

for x in &vector1 {
    println!("A reference to {}", x);
}
}
```

Chapter 11- Generics

When writing a function or a data type, sometimes, we may need it to work with many types of arguments. Rust allows us to do these using Generics. In type theory, generics are referred to as "parametric polymorphism", meaning that they are functions or types with multiple forms over a particular parameter.

The standard library for Rust provides us with a type, that is, Option<T> that is generic. This is shown below:

```
#![allow(unused_variables)]
fn main() {
enum Option<T> {
  Some(T),
  None,
}
}
```

The <T> option is an indication that we have a generic data type. When declaring an enum, once you see a T, the type should be substituted for same type that was used in the generic. The example given below shows how we can use Option<T> with extra type annotations:

```
#![allow(unused_variables)]
fn main() {
let p: Option<i32> = Some(10);

}
```

In type declaration, we say Option<i32>. This is similar to Option<T>. In this option, the T will have a value of i32. On right side of our binding, we have a Some<T>, in which T is 10. Since it is an i32, the two sides will match. In case they fail to match, we will get an error:

```
let p: Option<f64> = Some(10);
```

This is not an indication that we are unable to make an Option<T> that holds a f64. They should match up as shown below:

```
#![allow(unused_variables)]
fn main() {
let p: Option<i32> = Some(10);
let q: Option<f64> = Some(10.0f64);
}
```

The above is fine as we have one definition and multiple uses.

It is not a must for generics to be generic over only one type. Consider the example given below from the Rust's standard library, Result<T, E:

```
#![allow(unused_variables)]
fn main() {
enum Result<T, E> {
   Ok(T),
   Err(E),
}
}
```

In this case, it is generic over two types, that is, T and E. Note that you can use any capital letter that you like.
Generic Functions

We can follow the same syntax to write functions that take generic types. This is demonstrated below:

```
#![allow(unused_variables)]
fn main() {
fn anything<T>(p: T) {
   // Code for p.
}
}
```

Our syntax in the above case has two parts, with the <T> saying, "the function is generic over one type T", while the x: T simply says, "x has type T".

Multiple arguments may also have similar generic type as shown below:

```
#![allow(unused_variables)]
fn main() {
fn takes_two_similar_things<T>(x: T, y: T) {
  // ...
}
}
```

We can also write a version taking multiple types:

```
#![allow(unused_variables)]
fn main() {
fn two_things<T, U>(x: T, y: U) {
  // ...
}
}
```

Generic Structs

Generic types can also be stored in a struct. For example:

```
#![allow(unused_variables)]
fn main() {
struct Coordinate<T> {
  x: T,
  y: T,
}
let int_origin = Coordinate { x: 0, y: 0 };
let float_origin = Coordinate { x: 0.0, y: 0.0 };
}
```

The generic parameters are defined in the <T>, and the "x :T" is used in the type declaration. If you are in need of adding an implementation to the generic struct, the type parameter should be type parameter should be declared after "impl". This is shown below:

```
#![allow(unused_variables)]
fn main() {
struct Coordinate<T> {
    x: T,
    y: T,
}

impl<T> Coordinate<T> {
    fn swap(&mut self) {
        std::mem::swap(&mut self.x, &mut self.y);
    }
}
}
```

You are aware of generics that take nearly every type. These can be very useful various circumstances.

Chapter 12- Closures

In some cases, it becomes important for one to wrap up a function and free up variables for a better clarity and reuse. The free variables which may be used normally come from the enclosing scope and they are "closed over" when used in a function. This is where we get the name "closures" from and Rust supports an implementation of these.

The purpose of closures is to capture the enclosing environment. Below is a closure that helps in capturing the x variable:

|val| val + x

Below is an example of a closure:

```
#![allow(unused_variables)]
fn main() {
let add_one = |p: i32| p + 1;

assert_eq!(2, add_one(1));

}
```

We have created a binding, that is, add_one, and then we have added it to a closure. The arguments for the closure go between pipes (|), and the body itself is an expression, which is "p + 1" in our case. The {} is also an expression, so it is possible for us to have multi-line closures:

```
#![allow(unused_variables)]
fn main() {
let add_two = |p| {
  let mut result: i32 = p;

  result += 1;
  result += 1;
  result
```

```
};
assert_eq!(4, add_two(2));
}
```

You must have noticed that there are significant differences between closures and functions that are normally defined with the "fn" keyword. We did not want to annotate the types of the arguments that closure takes or the values that it returns. However, we can do the following:

```
#![allow(unused_variables)]
fn main() {
let add_one = |p: i32| -> i32 { p + 1 };

assert_eq!(2, add_one(1));

}
```

However, there is no need for us to do as shown above.

Also, the syntax between closures and functions is similar, but somehow different:

```
#![allow(unused_variables)]
fn main() {
fn  add_one_v1   (p: i32) -> i32 { p + 1 }
let add_one_v2 = |p: i32| -> i32 { p + 1 };
let add_one_v3 = |p: i32|        p + 1 ;

}
```

Here is another example of a closure:

```
fn main() {
   // Incrementing using closures and functions.
   fn  ourFunction      (x: i32) -> i32 { x + 1 }


   let closure_annotated = |x: i32| -> i32 { x + 1 };
```

```
    let closure_inferred = |x    |       x + 1 ;

    let x = 1;
    // Call the function and the closures.
    println!("ourFunction: {}", ourFunction(x));
    println!("closure_annotated: {}",
closure_annotated(x));
    println!("closure_inferred: {}",
closure_inferred(x));

    // A closure that takes no arguments and returns an
`i32`.
    // The return type has been inferred.
    let one = || 1;
    println!("A closure that returns one: {}", one());

}
```

This gives the following as the result:

```
ourFunction: 2
closure_annotated: 2
closure_inferred: 2
A closure that returns one: 1
```

Conclusion

This marks the end of this book. Rust is a programming language developed to be used for systems programming. This is a type of programming that involves the development of low-level applications, especially those that communicated with the hardware directly. Computer operating systems are examples of such applications. Rust takes the same syntax as C++, but its developers were in need of providing a better type safety while at the same time maintaining the performance. The good thing with Rust is that it is an open source programming language. Rust is also a good programming language for the development of highly concurrent systems. In Rust, there is no automatic garbage collection like in Go, Java etc. Instead of this, the management of memory and other resources are managed via resource acquisition with optional reference counting.